Making Healthy Decisions
Injury Prevention

Unit 1

BSCS

KENDALL/HUNT PUBLISHING COMPANY
4050 Westmark Drive   Dubuque, Iowa 52002

ADVISORY COMMITTEE
Lawrence W. Green
Donald C. Iverson
Lloyd J. Kolbe
Nathan Maccoby
Katharine G. Sommers

BSCS PROJECT STAFF
Nancy M. Landes, Project Director and Revision
Coordinator, Final Edition
James D. Ellis, Project Director, Field-test Edition
Rodger W. Bybee, Contributing Author
Joseph D. McInerney, Contributing Author
Susan Frelick Wooley, Contributing Author
Teresa T. Hendrickson, Editor, Field-test Edition
C. Yvonne Wise, Editor, Final Edition
Jan Girard, Art Coordinator
Byllee Simon, Senior Executive Assistant

WRITING TEAMS, FIELD-TEST EDITIONS
Katherine A. Corley, Middle School Teacher
Sandra L.H. Davenport, M.D.
Ann Junk, Middle School Teacher
Terry Shaw, Middle School Teacher
David R. Stronck, Health Educator
Gordon Thies, Health Educator
Gordon E. Uno, Science Educator

REVIEWERS, FIELD-TEST EDITIONS
Steven N. Blair
Glen Gilbert
Gilda Gussin
Louise Light
Peter D. Loranger
Richard R.J. Lauzon
Terry Shaw
David A. Sleet

BSCS ADMINISTRATIVE STAFF
Timothy H. Goldsmith, Chair, Board of Directors
Joseph D. McInerney, Director
Lawrence Satkowiak, Chief Financial Officer

FIELD-TEST SCHOOLS
Challenger Middle School, Colorado Springs,
Colorado
Aspen Middle School, Aspen, Colorado
Buffalo Ridge Elementary School, Grade 6,
Laramie, Wyoming
Calhan Elementary School, Grade 6, Calhan,
Colorado
Carver Elementary School, Grade 6, Colorado
Springs, Colorado
Kearney Middle School, Commerce City,
Colorado
Ortega Middle School, Alamosa, Colorado
Sabin Junior High School, Colorado Springs,
Colorado
Sproul Junior High School, Widefield, Colorado
Webster Elementary School, Grade 6, Widefield,
Colorado
Widefield Elementary School, Grade 6, Widefield,
Colorado
Watson Junior High School, Widefield, Colorado

ARTISTS/PHOTOGRAPHERS
Susan Bartle
Brenda Bundy
Carlye Calvin
Jan Girard
Nancy Smalls
Linn Trochim

ISBN 0-7872-1218-0

This work was supported by the Gates Foundation, the Helen K. and Arthur E. Johnson Foundation, the Piton
Foundation, and the Adolph Coors Foundation. However, the opinions expressed herein do not necessarily reflect
the position or policies of the funding agencies, and no official endorsement should be inferred.

10 9 8 7 6 5 4 3 2 1

TABLE OF CONTENTS

UNIT 1: INJURY PREVENTION

FOREWORD

Whether you are aware of it or not, you make decisions about your health all day, every day. You are making decisions about your health when you decide what to eat for breakfast or whether to eat breakfast at all, whether to brush and floss your teeth, whether to wear a safety belt if you ride to school in a car, how to communicate with your classmates and teachers once you arrive at school, what to eat for lunch, whether to participate in sports or exercise after school, which television programs you watch, and when you go to sleep. Believe it or not, just about everything you do has some impact on your health and YOU are in charge of most of those decisions. Are the decisions you make healthy ones? How do you know? Do you care?

Sometimes, it's tough to make healthy decisions. All of us have lots of excuses: It's not what my friends are doing. I'm not sick, so why worry about what I eat? I'm careful, so I'm not going to get hurt. I really don't have time to exercise. No one else in the car has on a safety belt. In the lessons you are about to experience, we hope to convince you that it makes sense to pay attention to your health while you're healthy. Although some of the actions you take might not have an effect until years later, many decisions will make a difference right now in how you feel, how you relate to your friends and family, whether or not you become injured, whether you contract a life-threatening illness, or whether you put someone else's life and health at risk.

We sincerely hope you enjoy the activities in this unit of *Making Healthy Decisions* and that they make a difference in how you care for yourself and those around you. Remember, the healthy decisions are up to you.

Nancy M. Landes
Revision Director

James D. Ellis
Project Director
Field-test Edition

v

INTRODUCTION TO INJURY PREVENTION

Have you ever heard someone say, "Well, accidents *will* happen," especially after someone has made a mistake? Do you believe that "accidents" just happen—that they are out of your control—or do you believe those events have causes? Do most injuries occur by "accident," or are there reasons for people's injuries? In this unit, you will investigate the answers to those and other questions as you learn about a very important health issue—preventing injuries to yourself and others.

Believe it or not, more young people in the United States die from injuries than from all diseases combined. Each year injuries cause more than 150,000 deaths and many more visits to the hospital. Many young people suffer permanent disabilities as a result of injuries that could have been prevented.

So, what can you do to prevent injuries? You can learn about the causes of injuries and how your actions can put you and others at risk of injury. You can learn skills that will help you act appropriately in emergency situations. You can learn how to make decisions that will keep you safe and lower your risk of injury. You can practice the behaviors, such as fastening your safety belt and wearing a helmet when biking, that protect you from injuries. You can also share with family members and friends the information and skills you learn in these lessons to keep them from becoming injury statistics.

Remember, "accidents"—and injuries—don't just happen. Find out the reasons why people become injured and work to change the behaviors and conditions that put people's live and health at risk. The life you save may be your own!

WHY INJURIES HAPPEN

The girls' basketball team plays its first game of the season tomorrow. Anne and Jocina, teammates on the Bombers, are outside practicing lay-ups and free throws. Anne's mother calls them to come inside for a phone call from their coach. As they race for the door, Anne misses a step and falls, spraining her ankle. No opening day game for Anne. What rotten luck! Or was bad luck involved at all?

ACTIVITY: WHAT DO YOU THINK CAUSES INJURIES?

Procedure

1. Read each case that follows.
2. Decide what you think caused the reported injuries.
3. In your notebook, explain in writing the cause (or causes) of the injuries in each case.

Case #1: John Stevens was injured after he rode his bike into an intersection and skidded to avoid being hit by a car. John rode into the intersection without stopping for the posted stop sign. John claimed that he was worried about a math test he had to take during second period, and he wasn't paying attention.

Case #2: Maria Martinez suffered a broken arm when the roof of her home collapsed during a tornado. The tornado killed seven local residents.

Case #3: Susan O'Brien received cuts on her face and hands when the sled she was riding nose-dived into a hole concealed during a recent snowfall. Since then, park officials have posted warning signs about hidden hazards in Greenmont Park.

Case #4: Jerome Washington seriously sprained his knee and ankle after he lost control of his skateboard on the expert run at the Woodlawn Skateboard Club. Jerome was wearing a protective helmet, knee pads, and elbow pads at the time of his fall. He began skateboarding less than a month before he was injured.

Case #5: James Moore suffered a concussion after he tripped on a rough piece of pavement and fell as he walked to his car in a well-lighted parking lot. Mr. Moore was on his way home after working an 18-hour shift at the local hospital.

Case #6: Debbie Green is recovering from head injuries she received in a recent automobile crash. She was driving at 35 mph when her car suddenly skidded on a patch of ice and then stopped. Ms. Green's car was not damaged except for the windshield that cracked when her head hit it. She was not wearing her safety belt at the time of the incident.

Stop and Discuss

1. What do you think caused each person's injuries?
2. How do your opinions compare with those of your teammates or classmates?
3. Which case was the most difficult to explain? Why was it the most difficult?

ACTIVITY: POSSIBLE REASONS FOR WHY INJURIES HAPPEN

Procedure

1. Read the six possible causes of injury that follow.
2. Review each of the six cases that you read in the previous activity.
3. Choose **one** of the following possible causes of injury that best describes what caused the injuries in each of the six cases. Write your choice in your notebook.
   Use the case number or the person's name to be clear about which cause you chose for which case.
4. Compare the explanation you wrote in the previous activity with the cause of injury you chose from the following list.
   How is your explanation the same or different from the cause you chose from the list?

Possible Causes of Injury

1. **Lack of Skill.** These injuries occur when people attempt activities that require more skill and ability than they have at that time.

2. **Environment.** Injuries caused by the environment occur during unfavorable conditions, such as rain, snow, floods, tornadoes, or earthquakes. People usually cannot control such conditions, but they can take safety precautions when such conditions occur.

3. **Being Tired or Ill.** Illness and fatigue (tiredness) often cause people to be less alert and to behave differently than they would usually behave. Conditions of fatigue or illness often slow a person's reaction time, sometimes causing injuries.

4.   **Emotions.** Strong emotions, such as sadness, anger, happiness, anxiety, fear, or jealousy, often cause people to pay less attention to what they are doing. Therefore, people who are experiencing strong emotions are not as likely to be careful and their carelessness can result in injuries.

5.   **Values.** A person's attitudes may affect his or her actions. Attitudes about what is important may cause people to choose certain safety precautions and to ignore others. People who believe that injuries never happen to them often take more risks. People who do not feel good about themselves or about others may ignore precautions that prevent injuries.

6.   **Lack of Knowledge.** Some injuries occur when people are not aware of possible dangers in their environment or situation. Because they are unaware of hazards, individuals take risks they wouldn't normally take.

ACTIVITY: CAUSES OF MY INJURIES

Procedure

1.   Copy the following chart onto a piece of notebook paper.
2.   Complete as much of the chart as you can.
      You might not have experienced injuries for all six causes. That is okay. Write about only those injuries you have experienced. Do not make up answers.
3.   Share your completed chart with a partner or with your teammates.
4.   Discuss ways you might have prevented your injuries.

I Experienced Injuries That Were Caused by:	This Is What Happened...	This Injury Might Have Been Prevented by:
Lack of Skill		
Environment		
Being Tired or Ill		
Emotions		
Values		
Lack of Knowledge		

WRAP UP

Look through two or three recent issues of your local newspaper, listen to radio broadcasts of the local news, or watch your local television newscast for two or three days. Cut out articles from each issue of the newspaper or take notes from radio or television news stories that report injuries.

Make a chart similar to the one you completed in the activity "Causes of my Injuries" but use the following headings: Injuries Reported in Newspapers [or on Radio or Television] That Were Caused by... and This Is What Happened... Then, use the information from the articles or newscasts and complete the chart.

Share your chart with your teacher and classmates and discuss how the injuries might have been prevented.

INVOLVING FAMILY MEMBERS

Take home your completed chart from the activity "Causes of My Injuries" or complete the assignment at home with the help of a parent or guardian. Suggest that each member of your family complete such a chart and compare the charts. Talk about ways each family member could have prevented his or her injuries.

Enlist the help of your family members in completing the Wrap Up assignments. Family involvement is important in preventing injuries.

HOW DEADLY ARE INJURIES?

According to the National Safety Council, heart disease is the leading cause of death in the United States, followed by cancer and strokes. In general, how old do you think a person who dies of heart disease might be? Four years old? Twenty-five years old? Fifty years old? Sixty-five years old? Although a person of any age could die from heart disease, especially if he or she were born with a heart problem, statistics show that most people will not die from heart disease until they are between 65 and 74 years of age. (People do die from heart disease at younger ages, but not in large numbers.)

So, what about you? If you don't have to worry about heart disease until you are quite a bit older, are you risk-free? Or, might statistics show that people your age die from other causes? What might those causes be? Can most deaths of people your age be prevented?

ACTIVITY: CHECKING THE NUMBERS

Procedure

1. Review the statistics presented in the data table How Did They Die?
2. Be prepared to answer the discussion questions that follow the data table.

How Did They Die?* (Based on Number of Deaths Reported in 1989)

Number of Deaths

Cause	Male	Female	Total
All Causes, 1 to 4 years			
Accidents	1,675	1,099	2,774
Motor Vehicle	548	457	1,005
Fires, Burns	355	253	608
Drowning	403	186	589
Ingestion of Food, Object	69	36	105
Mechanical Suffocation (from smothering, cave-ins, or strangulation)	45	34	79
Congenital Anomalies (Birth Defects)	437	491	928
Cancer	278	228	506
All Causes, 5 to 14 Years			
Accidents	2,718	1,372	4,090
Motor Vehicle	1,421	845	2,266
Drowning	402	113	515
Fires, Burns	252	215	467
Firearms	203	28	231
Mechanical Suffocation	82	13	95
Cancer	646	509	1,155
Homicide	300	210	510
All Causes, 15 to 24 Years			
Accidents	12,647	4,091	16,738
Motor Vehicle	9,429	3,512	12,941
Drowning	833	72	905
Firearms	471	45	516
Poison (solid, liquid)	376	111	487
Fires, Burns	204	105	309
Homicide	5,112	1,073	6,185
Suicide	4,106	764	4,870

*Source: National Safety Council. *Accident Facts, 1992 Edition.* (1992). Itasca, IL: National Safety Council, pp.6-7.

1. What is the leading cause of death of young people ages 1 to 24 in the United States?
2. Compare the number of deaths of males and females. Which causes of death are higher for males than for females? Why do you think this is the case?
3. Compare the number of deaths in similar categories of those ages 5 to 14 with those ages 15 to 24. Which causes of death take more lives in the 15-to-24 age range? Why do you think this is so?
4. Do you think you or your family members are at risk of death due to injuries from accidents. How could you prevent such injuries from happening?

ACTIVITY: CONSTRUCTING BAR GRAPHS

In this part of the lesson, you will construct three bar graphs using the data shown in the data table How Did They Die? Construct one bar graph for causes of death for those 1 to 4 years of age, a second for those 5-to-14 years of age, and a third for those 15-to-24 years of age. You might design your bar graphs so that they compare the total number of deaths from the various causes, or you might compare the number of deaths of males and females on each graph. (See sample bar graphs.) You can decide which sets of data to display.

Procedure

1. Review the data from the data table How Did They Die?
2. Decide which data you will use on your bar graphs to compare the causes of death of the three age groups.
3. Construct each bar graph by doing the following:
    a. Draw the "x" and "y" axes.
    b. Label each axis with words that indicate which variable that axis displays.
    c. Decide on the column labels along the "x" axis.
    d. Write the labels on the "x" axis, leaving adequate space between labels.
    e. Decide on the number scale for the "y" axis.
        (Hint: Find the highest and lowest numbers that you must represent on the graph and then decide on evenly spaced intervals for all the numbers in-between.)
    f. Write the number scale along the "y" axis, making sure that you space the numbers on the scale evenly.
    g. Draw the bars in the appropriate spaces on your graph.
    h. Give each graph a title so that you will know which graph is which.

Sample Bar Graphs

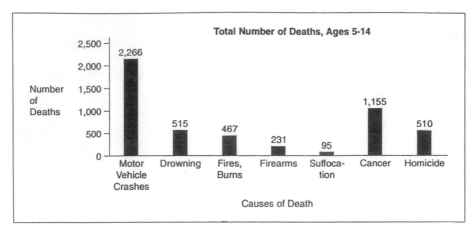

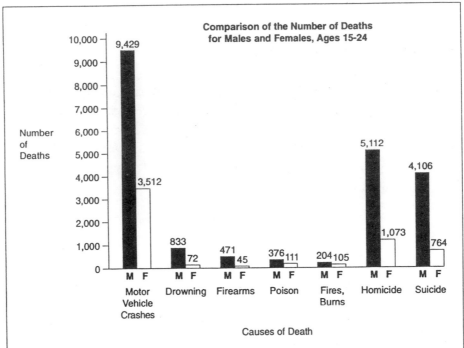

WRAP UP

Discuss the answers to the following questions with your teammates or classmates.

1. Which display of data—the data table or the bar graph—is better for displaying the information presented in this lesson? Why do you think so?
2. Why might injuries from accidents be the leading cause of death for people between the ages of 1 and 24?
3. How could you and your classmates help prevent the types of events listed in the data table How Did They Die?
4. How can you keep yourself from becoming a statistic in such a data table?

INVOLVING FAMILY MEMBERS

Take home a copy of the data table and the bar graphs you completed in class. Share the information with your family members. Talk about ways your family members could keep from becoming injured from the causes listed in the data table.

TAKING RISKS

Everyone takes risks. Some risks that people take are not likely to result in injury or death, but some risks are very dangerous. Such risks could lead to someone getting hurt or even killed. What kinds of risks do you take?

ACTIVITY: IDENTIFYING PERSONAL RISKS

Procedure

1. On notebook paper, write the letters a. through t. in one or two columns. Leave enough space following each letter to place a check mark and the description of the item.
2. Read the following list of items lettered a. through r. Decide which items are part of your life.
3. On your notebook paper, place a check mark beside the letter that corresponds to any item in the list that is a part of your life. Write the description of the item following each check mark.
    You do not have to write the description for any item that is not part of your life.
4. After letter s. and letter t. on your paper, write in an additional risk that you take in your life.
5. Review the items that you checked and the two you added. Of those items, circle the three that you think would be **most likely** to result in injuries or death.

a.____Riding a bicycle

b.____Playing sports

c.____Walking outside after dark

d.____Going up and down stairs

e.____Living with someone who smokes cigarettes

f.____Using power tools

g.____Riding on a skateboard or in-line skates

h.____Handling gasoline or kerosene

i.____Cooking

j.____Playing with matches

k.____Riding in an automobile without wearing a safety belt

l.____Getting into fights

m.____Handling a gun or a rifle

n.____ Swimming

o.____Riding on a motorcycle or a minibike

p.____Walking across streets

q.____Using a step ladder

r.____Living in a home that does not have a smoke detector

s._____

t._____

ACTIVITY: REDUCING MY RISKS

How might you reduce your risks of injury or death from risky activities? Do injuries just happen or could you do something to prevent them? To find out, complete the procedures that follow.

Procedure

1.　　Copy the following form three times onto a piece of notebook paper.
2.　　After each word "Risk," write one of the three risks that you circled in the previous activity "Identifying Personal Risks."
　　　Write each risk only once.
3.　　Under each risk, list two or three ways you could reduce your risk of injury.
　　　Think about what you could do to be more safe.

Risk:
I could reduce this risk by:
a.
b.
c.

Stop and Discuss

1.　　Of the three activities you listed, which activity do you think would be most risky for you? Why do you think so?

2.　　Are you still willing to accept the risks involved in that activity? Why or why not?

READING: PEER PRESSURE

Do you like to do things alone? Do you like to do things with other people? Have you ever done something with a group that you would never do alone? Have you ever felt forced to do something with a group that you really did not want to do?

People who are close to your own age are called **peers**. Your classmates are your peers. Your neighborhood friends are your peers. The influence of your peers on your behavior is called **peer pressure.**

Peer pressure can be helpful. It can get you to do things you would never do by yourself. For example, peer pressure might have encouraged you to take part in some school activities or to join a team or a club. The support of your friends often encourages you to have new, positive experiences.

Peer pressure also can be harmful. Sometimes it can persuade you to take risks that have a high potential for injury. For example, pressure from those around you might get you into a fight that you would never have started yourself. Or, it can push you to try activities that require skills better than you have. The following activity "Would I Do This Alone?" will encourage you to think about how peer pressure affects your life.

ACTIVITY: WOULD I DO THIS ALONE?

Procedure

1. Copy the following headings onto a piece of notebook paper and create a data table by drawing vertical lines between the headings.

I would do this alone.	**I would do this with others.**	**I would never do this.**

2. Read each action listed in the following chart.

3. On your paper, write each action under the appropriate heading. *You might write some actions under more than one heading.*

ACTIONS
Sing on stage.
Ride my bike on a busy street.
Ask adults to buckle their safety belts.
Skate down a steep hill while wearing in-line skates.
Ride on a motorcycle without a helmet.
Dive off a high diving board.
Walk through a cemetery at night.
Visit the principal in the office.

4.   Add some actions of your own choosing. List at least two additional actions you would take alone, two actions you would only take with others, and two actions you would never take.

5.   Share your data table with a partner and compare your lists. Would you be willing to do the same types of things alone or only with others? Is one of you willing to do some things the other person is not willing to do?

Stop and Discuss

1.   Which actions seem to be most affected by peer pressure?
2.   When has peer pressure ever influenced you to take a positive risk?
3.   When has peer pressure ever influenced you to take a risk with high potential for injury?
4.   Why do you think peer pressure is so strong for young people?

WRAP UP

Read the poem that follows and discuss these questions: What does this poem tell you about taking risks? How can you separate the positive risks form the negative ones? When are risks worth taking?

TO RISK

To laugh
      is to risk appearing the fool.
To weep
      is to risk appearing sentimental.
To reach out for another
      is to risk involvement.
To expose feelings
      is to risk exposing your true self.
To place your ideas, your dreams, before the crowd
      is to risk loss.
To love
      is to risk not being loved in return.
To live
      is to risk dying.
To hope
      is to risk despair.
To try at all
      is to risk failure.
But risk we must.
Because the greatest hazard in life
      is to risk nothing.

--Anonymous

INVOLVING FAMILY MEMBERS

Ask your family members to complete the activities from this lesson. How do people's attitudes toward taking risks change with age? How do the types of risks people take change with age? Do you and your parents or guardians agree on the types of risks that are acceptable for you?

WHO ARE YOUR ROLE MODELS?

Do you have a poster of a famous person hanging on a wall in your bedroom? Whose stickers or names do you display on your notebook? Are you wearing pins or other jewelry advertising someone famous? These displays could show others who your **role models** are.

A role model is a person whom you admire and try to be like in some way. Role models can be of the same or of the opposite gender. They can be younger, older, or of the same age.

You might know your role models personally, or you might only know about them. Role models do not deliberately try to teach you anything. Instead, they influence you by what they do and say. Sometimes people who have been selected by others as role models don't even know it. Many young people select famous people to be their role models.

We all have role models, whether we realize it or not. These are the people who help us decide what to be like. Do you know who your role models are?

ACTIVITY: IDENTIFYING ROLE MODELS

In this part of the lesson, you and your classmates will generate a list of possible role models.

Procedure

1. As your teacher shows you some pictures of famous people, write the names of those people in your notebook.
    Get help from your classmates if you do not know who some of the people are.
2. Discuss the following question with your classmates: Do you consider these people to be role models for people your age?
    In your discussion, there probably will be differences of opinion. Explain your opinion clearly and then find out the reasons why someone might not agree with you.
3. Add to your list the names of people whom you think are role models for people your age.
4. Share with your classmates the names you added.

ACTIVITY: A CLOSER LOOK AT A ROLE MODEL

Procedure

1. Select a role model to analyze.
    This person should be someone you admire. You may choose someone from the list your class generated in the previous activity, or you may choose someone who is not on the class list. Your role model doesn't have to be a famous person; your role model can be a relative or a friend—someone you know personally.
2. After you have selected your role model, copy the data table A Closer Look at My Role Model into your notebook.
    Be sure and leave enough space for each answer.
3. Complete the data table to the best of your ability.
    You might not be able to complete every item, but write what you think your role model would answer for each item. If you know other things that are important about your role model, add them to your list.
4. After you have completed the data table, write the following two sentences in your notebook and complete each one. **"I am like my role model because..." "I am not like my role model because..."**
    As you complete these sentences, you may write more than one reason why you are like or not like your role model.

Data Table
A Closer Look at My Role Model

MY ROLE MODEL'S NAME IS
I think my role model
likes
wishes for
dislikes
enjoys
has tried
respects
is concerned about
creates
resolves conflicts by
takes risks when
does not take risks when

Stop and Discuss

1. In what ways are you like your role model? In what ways are you different?
2. In what ways would you like to be more like your role model? In what ways are you glad that you are different?
3. In what ways does your role model influence your behavior or the way you look? Do you think these influences are positive or negative? Why do you think so?
4. If your role model displays a certain characteristic that you really admire, what might you do to show that characteristic?
5. Does your role model know how you feel about him or her? If your role model is someone you know personally, how might you tell him or her about your feelings?

READING: THE INFLUENCE OF ROLE MODELS ON BEHAVIOR

Research has shown that people your age often try to become like their role models. This can have positive results if the role model is someone who is respected and acts in responsible ways. Sometimes, however, this modeling behavior gets young people into trouble if the role model's behavior is less than admirable. It all depends on who the role model is.

Sometimes, students select role models who are not real. Those role models might be actresses or actors who are playing a role in a carefully planned world. Sometimes young people forget this and then try to imitate something they have seen on television or in the movies. That kind of imitation can lead to trouble or can have unexpected results out in the "real world."

As you learned in the previous lesson, part of growing up involves learning to take more risks. Some risks are physical; other risks are social. Some risks are even emotional. Some risks you might feel comfortable taking by yourself; others you should never take by yourself or even with others. Making these decisions is not always easy. Having role models to look up to and to imitate can help you take the kinds of risks that will help you grow into an independent, responsible adult.

ACTIVITY: MY IDEAL ROLE MODEL

Although no one is perfect, some people make better role models than others because they display characteristics and actions that many people respect and admire. If you could invent an ideal role model, what characteristics would that person have? How would he or she think? How would this person look and act? What would be important to him or her? In this activity, you will have a chance to make some of those choices.

Procedure

1. In your notebook, write the heading My Ideal Role Model.
2. Think about someone who would make an ideal role model for you.
   Remember, this does not have to be a real person you have heard of or someone you know.
3. Under the heading, list at least 10 things that describe this ideal person.
4. When you have completed your list, share your ideas with a partner or with your cooperative team members.
5. If you agree that any characteristic listed by your partner(s) would fit your ideal role model, add that characteristic to your list.

Stop and Discuss

1. What are the most important qualities of your ideal role model?
   How do these qualities compare with those listed by others in the class?
2. How is the ideal role model you described in this activity similar to the real role model you selected in the previous activity "A Closer Look at a Role Model?"
   How are they different?

3. If your real-life role model doesn't have all the qualities of your ideal role model, does this mean you should change your real-life role model? Why or why not?
4.. Has acting like your role model ever encouraged you to take risks that helped you grow or to take risks where you might have become injured? Explain your answer.
5. Do actors or actresses differ in real life from the characters they play on the screen? How might this be confusing for someone who has selected a particular television or movie character as a role model?

WRAP UP

Believe it or not, there is probably a younger person out there who has chosen you as a role model. That person might be a younger brother or sister, or you might not even know the person. Younger students look to you for guidance about simple things, such as how to dress and how to wear their hair. They also look to you for clues about more important things, such as how to behave and how to treat other people.

In your notebook, write about how this news makes you feel. What qualities do you have that would make you a good role model for a younger student? What characteristics do you have or what behaviors do you display that you would not want a younger student to imitate? How might you behave differently if you knew that a younger person were going to imitate you?

Whenever you are around younger students, think about your answers to the questions in the Wrap Up. Are you the kind of role model you would like to be?

INVOLVING FAMILY MEMBERS

Ask your parents or guardians about their role models when they were growing up. Whom did they admire? Whose posters did they display? Why did they choose those people? Were those people famous or people whom they knew?

Then, ask them who their role models are today. Whom do they admire? Have their role models changed? If they have changed, ask them why their role models are different now.

Share your choices of role models with your parents or guardians. Tell them what qualities you admire in your role models.

WHAT CAN YOU DO TO PREVENT INJURIES?

In the previous lessons, you learned that injuries don't just happen. Personal injuries have causes, and most injuries can be prevented. Besides staying home and never going any place or doing anything, can you keep from being injured? Can you still have fun and stay safe from injuries? The answers to both questions are **YES,** but you have to be aware and willing to take action to prevent injuries.

ACTIVITY: OUR IDEAS FOR PREVENTING INJURIES

Procedure

1. Review the causes of deaths due to injuries from the data table How Did They Die? in Lesson 2.
    The leading causes of deaths due to injuries were motor vehicle crashes, which include collisions between vehicles, collisions between motor vehicles and pedestrians, and collisions between motor vehicles and bicyclists.
2. With your teammates or partner, select the two causes for which you would most like to prevent injuries.
    If you select the cause "motor vehicle crashes," you can concentrate on one of the subcategories involving pedestrians or bicyclists, or you can think about all types of motor vehicle crashes.
3. At the top of a page in your notebook, write one of the causes of injures that you selected.
4. Brainstorm the things people could do to prevent injuries from that cause.
5. Review your list from step 4 and select the two or three suggestions that you think would prevent the most injures from that cause.
6. Repeat steps 3 through 5 for the second cause of injures you selected.
7. When all teams are ready, share your best suggestions with your classmates and teacher.

ACTIVITY: WHAT CONTRIBUTES TO INJURIES?

Procedure

1. Read the following story "A Trip to the Grocery Store."
2. List everything that contributed to Cheryl's head injury.
    Think about all the conditions and actions that were part of the process of Cheryl's injury. For example, the wet pavement probably contributed to Cheryl's head injury.

A Trip to the Grocery Store

Cheryl's father asked her to go to the nearby grocery store and pick up a few things he needed for dinner that evening. Cheryl decided to ride her bike to the store because it would take her too long to walk there and back. She took her backpack along because her bike doesn't have a basket. She knew that she could not carry the groceries in her arms and have control of her bike at the same time. Cheryl decided that she didn't need to wear her helmet because it wasn't far to the store.

Cheryl rode to the grocery store, bought the groceries, put them in her backpack, and started to ride home. Just then, it started to rain. Cheryl decided to ride a little faster so she could get home quickly. As she approached the first intersection, Cheryl did not see the stop sign that was hidden behind a large tree branch. She kept pedaling as fast as she could.

When she reached the intersection, she saw the stop sign and the car that was approaching the intersection from her left. She put on her brakes, but her narrow bike tires skidded on the wet pavement, and she fell. As she fell, she hit her head on the curb and was knocked unconscious. The driver of the car stopped to help, but he did not know first aid and wasn't sure what to do. By that time, another driver also had stopped, so the first driver drove quickly to the grocery store and called 911 for an ambulance.

The paramedics arrived in time, administered first aid, and took Cheryl to the hospital. She was hospitalized for four days and could not go back to school for two weeks because she had a severe concussion.

READING: WORKING TOGETHER TO PREVENT INJURIES

Look at the list your class made when you discussed what contributed to Cheryl's head injury. Your list probably included a number of different things, such as Cheryl not wearing her bicycling helmet, the rain which made the pavement wet, and the branch that hid the stop sign. Each of those things that had something to do with Cheryl's injury is called a **factor**. (A factor is anything that contributes to a result or a process.)

People who study injuries and their causes often group the factors that contribute to injuries into three categories:

(1)   the human factors,
(2)   the environmental factors, and
(3)   the technological or physical factors.

Usually, injuries result from a combination of all three types of factors. No helmet on Cheryl's head was a human factor because she made the decision not to wear her helmet. The rain that made the pavement wet was an environmental factor. The branch that hid the stop sign was considered a physical factor. The tree grew in such a way that one of its branches hid the stop sign.

Although all three types of factors can contribute to a person's injuries, the human factors are the ones we can control. For example, even though Cheryl did not cause the rain and she could not do anything about the rain, what could she have done that might have prevented her injury? That's right. She could have ridden her bike more slowly so that she would have been less likely to skid on the wet pavement.

What about the branch that covered the stop sign? Although the branch is not a human factor, someone who trims trees for the city should have noticed the problem and trimmed the branch, or someone who drives by that intersection regularly might have called the city office and reported the problem. Some adults spend their working time thinking about the places where injuries occur. How can they make those environments safer? People can't change the weather, but they can improve road surfaces, or snow removal services, or decide when people should not drive on snow-covered or flooded roads, for example. People concerned about environmental factors also look at information about injuries that do occur. If a lot of injuries happen to pedestrians at a certain intersection or stretch of road, the city engineers might put in a sidewalk or a crosswalk that separates the pedestrians from the traffic on the roadway. That way, pedestrians will be less likely to be injured in that location.

Other people work on solving the problems involving the physical or technological factors. Those people work mainly in manufacturing as engineers, product designers, factory workers, and maintenance personnel so that the products we use are as safe as possible. For example, some people work on preventing injuries from falls by designing and producing bathtub surfaces that are less slippery when they are wet. Other people work on inventions, such as air bags, that help protect people in a car crash. Other people design and manufacture toys that do not have sharp edges or points or small pieces on which children could choke. Although environmental and physical factors contribute to injuries, the prevention of injuries depends on people being aware, showing concern, and working together to solve problems.

Stop and Discuss

1. Review your answers to the previous Stop and Discuss questions.
    Classify your responses from question #1—What contributed to Cheryl's head injury?—into the three categories you just learned about: (1) the human factors, (2) the environmental factors, and (3) the physical or technological factors.
2. Discuss the three types of factors and give examples of each.

WRAP UP

Review the suggestions you wrote for preventing injuries in the first activity "Our Ideas for Preventing Injuries." Now that you know that injuries can be prevented three ways—by helping people make decisions that will protect them from injuries (human factors), by improving environmental conditions (environmental factors), and by improving physical and technological factors, suggest additional ways for preventing injuries from the causes you selected in the first activity.

After you have added to your list, choose your best suggestion from either cause of injuries and design a poster or cartoon that shows how injuries could be prevented from that cause.

INVOLVING FAMILY MEMBERS

Discuss with your family members the three types of factors that contribute to injuries. Talk about an injury that a family member received and decide what the human, environmental, and physical factors were that contributed to that injury. How could the injury have been prevented? (Use the three types of factors to help you decide how the injury could have been prevented.)

LESSON 6

WHO WEARS SAFETY BELTS?

Review the data table How Did They Die? from Lesson 2. What type of accident causes the highest number of deaths for all children and young adults, ages 1 through 24? How could many of those deaths have been prevented?

Think about your own behavior. Do you buckle your safety belt **every time** you get into a motor vehicle? Do your family members **always** buckle up and place infants and young children in safety seats before they head out on the road, even if it's just as far as the grocery store? If you answered yes to both questions, then you and your family are part of a growing number of Americans who always buckle up on matter how far they are traveling.

Although the number of people who always buckle up is increasing, only 50 percent of adults overall wear their safety belts every time they drive. The percentage is a little higher—up to 55 percent—in states that do not have such laws. If the safety belt laws are mandatory, then doesn't everyone have to buckle up? Why do some people still not wear safety belts, even though it's the law?

In this lesson, you will find out about safety belts and air bags and how they protect people in a motor vehicle crash. You also will conduct interviews to find out why some people buckle up all of the time and why others do not. Then, you will design strategies that might encourage people to use their safety belts every time they get into a motor vehicle.

READING: WHAT HAPPENS IN A CRASH?

Motor vehicle safety experts study crashes of motor vehicles both in laboratories and in real life to find out exactly what happens to the vehicle and to the people in it during a crash. They have examined all kinds of crashes: Front-end and rear impacts, cars that have been hit from the side, cars and trucks that have rolled over or flipped end over end. In their studies, the experts have found that there is not just one collision in a motor vehicle crash. There are actually **three** collisions: (1) the car's collision, (2) the human collision, and (3) the human body's internal collision.

The Car's Collision

The first collision causes the car to buckle and bend as it hits something and comes to an abrupt stop. In a frontal crash with a stationary object, such as a tree or a wall, at a speed of 30 miles per hour, the front end of the car crushes about two feet. The car comes to a complete stop within 1/10 of a second. The crushing of the front end absorbs some of the force of the crash and cushions the rest of the car. As a result, the passenger compartment comes to a more gradual stop than the front of the car and is relatively undamaged by the crash.

The Human Collision

The second collision is the "human" collision as the people in the car hit some part of the vehicles or each other. It is this human collision that causes injury.

At the moment of impact, people who are not wearing safety belts are still traveling at the original speed of the vehicle. After the vehicle comes to a complete stop, these unbelted people will slam into the steering wheel, or into the windshield, or into some other part of the inside of the vehicle. This is the human collision.

Another form of human collision is "person-to-person." Many serious injuries are caused by unbelted people colliding with each other. In a crash, the people in the vehicle tend to move toward the point of impact, not away from it. People in the front seat are often struck by rear-seat passengers who have become high-speed projectiles. Occupants bump heads, sometimes with fatal force. Children held on an adult's lap are crushed against the dashboard. In a side collision, a person can crash into nearby passengers and force them out the window or door.

Just how serious is the human collision? Imagine taking a brisk walk and running head first into a steel post! Such a collision would be about a 3 or 4 mile-per-hour collision. You probably would survive without serious injury, but it would not be a pleasant experience. Now imagine that you are running as fast as you can and again run head first into the steel post! This would be about a 15-mile-per-hour collision. This time, your injuries are likely to be serious. Now imagine striking that post at 30 miles per hour. The chances for survival would be poor at best. In a 30-mile-per-hour crash, a person in a vehicle strikes the interior of the car with a force of several thousand pounds. Imagine what happens in a 60 mile-per-hour crash!

A lot of people think that they are strong enough to brace themselves in a crash. They aren't. At 35 miles per hour, an unbelted person weighing 180 pounds would hit the steering wheel, the dashboard, or even the pavement outside the car with a force greater than 3,600 pounds. Nobody's arms are that strong!

The Internal Collision

Even after an unbelted person's body comes to a complete stop inside the motor vehicle, the person's internal organs are still moving forward. Suddenly, these organs hit other organs or the person's own bones. This third collision—the internal body collision—often causes considerable, and potentially fatal, injuries.

When the head collides with the windshield or dashboard, the brain hits the inside of the skull. The result may be only a mild concussion, but in many cases, blood vessels break or the brain is bruised and torn. These injuries to the brain can cause permanent brain damage. Of the known causes of epilepsy, head trauma, such as that received in an automobile crash, is one of the most frequently identified.

An unbelted person also is at serious risk of spinal cord injury in a motor vehicle crash. in fact, motor vehicle crashes account for about 45 percent of all spinal cord injuries reported. Almost one-third of these type of spinal cord injuries results in partial paralysis.

What About Air Bags?

Air bags are meant to help protect a person in a motor vehicle crash. Air bags do not take the place of safety belts, however. The bags cannot keep a person in the seat if the person is not wearing a safety belt. The safety belt keeps a person in place so that the air bag can cushion the person's head, face, neck, and chest—the parts of the body that are most likely to be injured in a crash.

The air bag is hidden in the steering wheel or dashboard until it is needed. When a crash sets off the sensors, harmless nitrogen gas inflates the bag. It all happens faster than the blink of an eye—in less than one tenth of a second. The bag quickly deflates after it has been inflated.

When an air bag inflates, it sends out a puff of talcum powder that is used to lubricate the bag so that it releases smoothly. The powder might look like smoke, but it is harmless and disappears quickly.

Can air bags protect people in all kinds of crashes? Actually, air bags are designed to work in head-on or near-head-on collisions. They will not inflate if the car is struck from the rear or from the side. That's another reason why it's important to have those safety belts fastened. You cannot predict from which direction your car might be hit.

Stop and Discuss

1. Explain the three collisions in your own words.
2. Is it safe to hold a child on your lap and put the safety belt around both of you? Why or why not?
   Think about the information from The Human Collision.
3. Why is it important for a driver to wear a safety belt even if the car is equipped with a driver's side air bag?

ACTIVITY: WHAT'S YOUR EXCUSE?

Most people know that people who wear safety belts are less likely to be injured or killed in a motor vehicle crash. So, why don't more people buckle up? What are their excuses? In this activity, you and your classmates will do some research to find out why some people do and why some people don't buckle up.

Procedure

1. Using the interview forms your teacher provides, interview three people of different ages and find out if they use safety belts and how often they use them.
    If possible, interview one adult, one teenager, and one child who is between the ages of 7 and 10.
2. Record on the interview forms the answers that people give you for each of the questions.
3. Bring your results to class.
4. Compare your results with those of your classmates.
5. Make a list of the reasons people gave for not buckling up all of the time.

Stop and Discuss

1. Do more adults, teenagers, or children use their safety belts all of the time?
2. Analyze the reasons people gave for not wearing safety belts. Do you think their reasons are valid? Why or why not?
3. How many people mentioned that their cars have automatic safety belts (passive restraints) or air bags? Do you think having the automatic safety belts increases the use of safety belts in general? Why or why not?
4. How many people whose cars are equipped with air bags also fasten their safety belts?
5. Do you think more people would wear safety belts if someone in the car asked them to do so? In what situations might you feel comfortable asking others to wear their safety belts? In what situations might you feel uncomfortable asking others to wear their safety belts?

READING: REASONS FOR NOT WEARING A SAFETY BELT

In a study conducted in 1984, 250 sixth and seventh grade students were asked whether or not they used safety belts. Only 20 of them (8 percent) said they used safety belts **all** of the time. Fourteen students (about 6 percent) said they used safety belts at least half of the time when they rode in cars. The rest of the students—216 of them (86 percent)—reported that they wore safety belts less than half of the time or not at all. In fact, 84 students (about 34 percent) said they **never** used safety belts.

The following are the reasons those students gave for not wearing safety belts all of the time:

- ☮ Not in the habit
- ☮ Don't think about it
- ☮ Uncomfortable to wear
- ☮ Takes too much time to put on
- ☮ Inconvenient to use
- ☮ Not necessary for short trips
- ☮ Don't like to feel confined
- ☮ Afraid of being trapped in a car if in an accident
- ☮ Don't want to be bothered
- ☮ Don't expect to be in an accident anyway
- ☮ Will not keep me from getting hurt if in a bad crash
- ☮ Friends would make fun of me
- ☮ Don't know how safety belts work
- ☮ Not "cool"
- ☮ Makes me think about getting in a crash
- ☮ Parents haven't asked me to

Compare those results with a 1990 nationwide survey of high school students, grades 9-12. In that survey, about 24 percent of the students said that they wore safety belts every time they rode in a car or truck. Twenty-three percent of the students reported that they never wore safety belts. That means that about 40 percent of the students probably wore safety belts "some of the time."

ACTIVITY: DO STUDENTS AT YOUR SCHOOL WEAR SAFETY BELTS?

Conduct a survey of your own at school and find out what percentage of the students wear their safety belts all of the time, some of the time, or not at all.

Procedure

1. As a class, decide how you will conduct a survey of students at your school.
   You might interview students during the lunch period, before or after school, or during certain class periods if you get the teachers' permission. Or, you could design a written survey, hand it out to the students, and ask them to complete the survey and turn it in to you or your teacher.
2. Decide how many students you will survey.
   *You do not have to interview every student in the school to find out what percentage of the students always, sometimes, or never wear safety belts. You can use a **random sample** of students to represent all of the students in the school.*
3. Design your survey.
   In your survey, find out how many of your classmates do or do not wear safety belts every time they ride in a motor vehicle. For those classmates who answer that they do not wear safety belts all of the time, ask them for their reasons for not wearing their safety belts.
4. Conduct the survey and record your results.

Stop and Discuss

1. Compare the information from your school survey with the information reported in 1984 and in 1990. Do more students in your school wear safety belts now than the students did in 1984? in 1990? Are the reasons for not wearing safety belts the same or different from the 1984 survey results?

2. Compare the reasons people gave in the activity "What's Your Excuse?" to the reasons given by the students in your school and the students in the 1984 survey. Are students' and adults' reasons the same or different? Are you surprised by any of the results?

3. How do the 1990 survey results of high school students relate to the data you reviewed in Lesson 2, How Deadly Are Injuries?

4. Since 1984, a lot of time and money have been spent on advertisements in magazines, on the radio, and on television to encourage people to wear safety belts. Based on the results of your surveys, do you think those advertisements have been successful? Why or why not? How might the advertisements be more successful?

ACTIVITY: LET'S ENCOURAGE SAFETY BELT USE

Now you know people's reasons for not wearing safety belts. How would you encourage people to change their behavior so that they use safety belts every time they drive or ride in a motor vehicle? How might you convince parents to always buckle their small children into child safety seats?

Procedure

1. With a partner or teammates, brainstorm some ways you might encourage people to use their safety belts.
    Think about the reasons people gave for not using their safety belts. What would convince people to change their minds about using safety belts?

2. Decide on one strategy that you think would work best.

3. Share your team's best strategy with your classmates.

4. As a class, rank order the "best" strategies.

5. With your partner or teammates, select one "best" strategy to try on a family member or a friend who does not usually wear a safety belt.

6. Try the strategy.

7. Be prepared to share your results with your classmates.

1. Which strategies worked? Which did not? Why do you think some strategies worked and others did not?
2. Who are more difficult to convince to wear safety belts: adults, teenagers, or children? Why do you think this group is more difficult to convince?
3. Is it easy to get people to change their behavior? Why or why not?

WRAP UP

Your teacher will divide your class into small groups and will ask each group to read and discuss one of the following situations. As a group, decide on a solution to the person's problem and be prepared to report your solution to the class.

Situation 1: You are riding as a back-seat passenger and your best friend's father is driving. As you start, you can only find one-half of your safety belt, and it looks like it hasn't been used in ages. You can't find the other half, so you can't buckle up. You ask your friend's father where the other half is, and he says, "I have no idea. You'll be all right. We're only going to the park." What should you do?

Situation 2: You've gone to a basketball game to meet a group of friends. Some of them are in high school and one of them has just gotten her driver's license. After the game, she says, "Hey, let's all pile into my car and go get something to eat." When you get to the car and everyone starts "piling in," you realize you're in a front seat with several other people. There's no way you or anyone else, besides the driver, can buckle any safety belts. What do you do?

Situation 3 : You're invited out to the movies by a new group of friends. When they pick you up, you get in the front seat. The driver is not wearing a safety belt, and neither is anyone else. You reach for your safety belt and the driver looks at you and says, "What's the matter? Don't you trust my driving?" The others wait for you to answer. What do you do?

Situation 4: Imagine that you have gotten your driver's license. You've invited some friends to go to the beach. Everyone gets in the car, eager to go, talking and laughing, but no one buckles a safety belt. This is the first time you've been allowed to drive your friends anywhere in a car. What do you do?

With your group, design a poster that would convince someone to buckle up. Display the class posters in the hallway, at a PTA meeting or parent/teacher night, or in a popular community location, such as a shopping mall or a movie theater.

INVOLVING FAMILY MEMBERS

Make a safety agreement with your family members. Your agreement could look something like this:

You:

I agree to take actions to keep safe. I will always use my safety belt, and I will not use alcohol or other drugs. I will find another ride or call you rather than ever ride with a drinking or drug-taking driver. If I ride a bicycle or ride on a motorcycle, I promise that I will wear a helmet. I recognize that you care about what happens to me, and I will keep this agreement.

_____
Signature, Date

Parent or Guardian:

I agree to take actions to keep safe. I will always use my safety belt. If I choose to drink, I will not drive myself and I will only ride with a sober driver. I will find another ride or call a taxi rather than ever ride with a drinking or drug-taking driver. If I ride a motorcycle or bicycle, I promise that I will wear a helmet. I recognize that you care about me, and I will keep this agreement.

_____
Signature, Date

HELPING OTHERS TO PREVENT INJURIES

So far in this unit, you have been learning about the importance of preventing injuries and some ways you might prevent personal injuries by learning the causes of unintentional injuries, by taking fewer risks, and by paying attention to the human, environmental, or physical factors involved in injuries. In the second activity of this lesson, you will have a chance to share your knowledge about preventing injuries with some special people—younger students—who really look up to you for advice and as role models.

ACTIVITY: WHAT DO YOU KNOW ABOUT PREVENTING INJURIES?

Students your age and younger are at particular risk for injuries as pedestrians, as bicycle riders, and—believe it or not—at home. How can you help students your age and younger prevent injuries as they walk to and from school or around the neighborhood? What injury-prevention strategies can you suggest for students who ride bikes? How can you help others prevent injuries at home? You will figure out answers to these questions as you complete this lesson. First, find out what you already know about preventing injuries as a pedestrian, as a bicyclist, and at home.

<u>Preventing Injuries to Pedestrians</u>

Before you can help someone else prevent injuries, you need to be sure you know some "rules of the road" yourself. Make sure you've got your facts straight before you share them with others.

Procedure

1. At the top of a piece of notebook paper, write the title Pedestrian True or False.
2. In a vertical column at the left-hand side of the paper, write the numbers 1 through 10. *Leave two or three lines between the numbers.*
3. Read the first statement under the heading Pedestrian True or False.
4. Decide whether the statement is true or false and reasons why you think the statement is true or false.
5. Write T (true) or F (false) beside the corresponding number on your paper, according to whether you think the statement is true or false.
6. In a few words or sentences, explain why you think the statement is either true or false.
7. Read the next statement.
8. Repeat steps 4 through 7 for each of the ten statements.

Pedestrian True or False

1. A pedestrian is a person who rides a horse.
2. Young people have a high pedestrian death rate.
3. Elderly people have a low pedestrian death rate.
4. If there is no sidewalk, pedestrians should walk on the left side of the road so they can see oncoming traffic.
5. Small children prefer to cross the street in the middle of the block.
6. People using crosswalks never get killed.
7. Wet roads do not increase the likelihood of pedestrian injuries.
8. Girls have a higher pedestrian injury rate than boys.
9. Most pedestrian injuries and deaths of children ages 1 through 14 happen during daylight hours.
10. The first motor vehicle death in the U. S. was a person stepping out of a streetcar.

Stop and Discuss

1. What are some behaviors that children might practice that would help them to prevent injuries as pedestrians?
2. What strategies might you use to make children aware of those behaviors and to encourage them to adopt the behaviors that will prevent injuries?
3. How many of the behaviors that you listed in answer to question #1 do you follow (a) all of the time, (b) some of the time, or (c) seldom or never? How would you rate yourself as a pedestrian role model for younger children?.

Preventing Injuries to Bicyclists

Bicycles are the most common form of transportation for those too young to drive a car. Almost all children have some kind of wheeled vehicle that gets them around the neighborhood. One study reported that almost one-half of all Americans—children and adults—ride bicycles regularly.

We all know that bicycle riding can be fun. It also promotes physical fitness by making your heart and lungs work harder and by strengthening your legs. Bicycle riding also can be the cause of injuries if people do not wear helmets, ride safely, or keep their bicycles in good repair. In one study of hospital emergency room visits, health workers found that more than one of every 80 elementary school-age children (ages 6-12) required hospital treatment for a bicycle injury not involving a motor vehicle. How can you keep yourself and others from becoming bicycle injury statistics?

Procedure

1.   Follow the same procedures in completing Bicycling True or False as you did in completing Pedestrian True or False.

Bicycling True or False

1. Legally, bicyclists can ride their bicycles on the sidewalk in a business area.
2. A bicyclist should obey the same traffic signs, lights, and signals as drivers of motor vehicles do.
3. Pedestrians have the right-of-way in crosswalks.
4. Bicyclists should walk their bicycles across heavily traveled streets at the crosswalk.
5. Riding at night is considered safe as long as a bicyclist has either a headlight or a rear reflector.
6. It is safe and proper to carry a passenger on a bicycle.
7. Hitching a ride by holding on to the bumper of a moving vehicle is safe as long as a bicyclist is careful.
8. It is best to ride three abreast when riding in a group.
9. Bicyclists should use proper hand signals every time they make a turn or stop.
10. On a country road, bicyclists should ride on the left side of the road facing oncoming traffic.
11. A bicycling helmet is the best protection against serious injuries when riding a bicycle.

Stop and Discuss

1. Are there environmental factors that could be changed to make bicycling safer in your neighborhood and in the school area? What recommendations could you make that would prevent potential injuries to bicycle riders?
2. Picture a bowling ball on a hospital bed with wheels. Now, think about this bed rolling downhill on a city street, gaining speed, and the ball falling off, crashing onto the pavement. Imagine what that crash would sound like and look like. How is this image similar to one of a bicyclist riding down a hill? How is the bowling ball like the cyclist's head? What if the bowling ball were filled with a soft substance, something like a brain? What could protect the bowling ball and its insides from serious injury?
3. Do you wear a helmet when you ride a bicycle? Why or why not? How can you convince younger students to wear a helmet when they ride their bicycles?
4. How many injury-prevention strategies for bicycling do you follow (a) all of the time, (b) some of the time, or (c) seldom or never? How would you rate yourself as a bicyclist role model for younger children?

Preventing Injuries at Home

According to the National Safety Council, at least one injury will occur at home in this country in the time it takes you to read this sentence. In the United States, someone is injured at home every 10 seconds and someone dies of injuries received at home every 26 minutes. This means that two people will die and 360 people will be injured at home in the next hour. Over time, you will find that approximately 8,600 injuries and 56 deaths occur at home every day, which translates into 60,200 injuries and 390 deaths every week and about 3,130,000 injuries and 20,300 deaths every year from injuries received at home. Most of these injuries and deaths **can** be prevented.

How can you emphasize the prevention of injuries at home? First, you need some information about your home before you can prescribe any safety remedies. In this part of the lesson, you will complete a "Home Injury-Prevention Survey" and decide where you and your family members can make some changes that might help prevent injuries at home. (You will not have to share your survey with anyone else in class. The purpose of this survey is to create personal and family awareness of injury-prevention strategies, not to compare the specific conditions of different families' homes.)

Procedure

1.	Take home the Home Injury-Prevention Survey that your teacher gives you.
2.	Read through the survey with one or more family members.
3.	Either by yourself or with family members, walk through your home and look carefully at the areas or items mentioned in the survey.
4.	Answer each question with a yes, or no, or does not apply to my home.
5.	Discuss the results with your family members and decide if there are steps you might take that will prevent potential injuries at home.

1.　　List five things that would help prevent potential injuries in your home. Are the things you listed human, environmental, or physical factors?
2.　　Why don't people take the injury-prevention precautions that they should in their homes?
3.　　How can you help younger children make injury prevention a priority in their homes?

ACTIVITY: DEVELOPING A PLAN OF ACTION TO HELP OTHERS PREVENT INJURIES

Now that you have reviewed ways to prevent injuries as a pedestrian, as a bicyclist, and at home, how can you share this information with younger children and encourage them to behave safely in those situations? This will be your next task in the lesson: prepare some activities or lessons about preventing injuries as pedestrians, as bicyclists, or at home that you will present to younger students.

Think about the activities you have completed in this unit and about the discussions with your classmates and teacher. Have any of the activities or discussions helped you think differently about risky actions you take now or might take in the future? If so, those might give you some ideas about how to prepare activities and discussion questions for younger students. Remember, in preparing activities for younger students, you should think about what will motivate those students to act in ways that will prevent injuries to themselves and others.

Often, just presenting information, even if you present it in an interesting way, is not enough to motivate someone to behave differently. You will need to involve the younger students actively in developing and practicing skills, such as making the appropriate hand signals when they ride a bicycle or making a map of the safest route to and from school. Keep in mind that your ultimate goal is to help the younger students prevent injuries to themselves and others; you want the children to choose safe behaviors and to make healthy decisions.

What follows are some suggestions for activities you can do with younger students. You do not have to choose these ideas; you might have better ones, but these will get you started. Be creative and have fun!

Suggestions for Helping Younger Students Prevent Injuries as Pedestrians

1.　　What's the Safest Way To and From School?

Where are the crosswalks in the area near the school? How often do the students use them? What could be done to reduce the risk of the students being injured while they cross the streets as they walk to and from school? (Think about both human and environmental factors.) First, make your own sample street map of the area around the school that is as accurate as possible. (You might adapt the appropriate portion of a city map, if one is available.) Next, make a transparency of your map so for demonstration purposes during the lesson, if necessary. Your map might look something like this one.

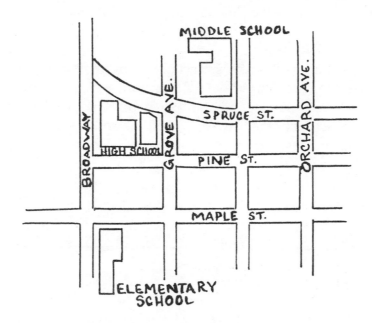

During the lesson, have the students use drawing paper or graph paper and draw a map showing the streets they travel to get to and from school. (With very young students, you might want to use copies of your map outline and let them fill in the route they usually take to and from school. Older students might be able to construct their own maps.)

After the students have constructed their maps, show them how to label the official, marked crosswalks found on the map with a green crayon or marker. Then, ask them to use a red marker or crayon and draw in any unofficial locations that they or other students often use when they cross the streets shown on the map.

Next, hold a discussion with the students. Ask them such questions as: What areas around the school seem to have a lot of unofficial crossing places? (Check the students' maps to see if they have indicated those areas in red.)

Why do you think students take the risk of crossing at unmarked places instead of at a crosswalk? (They might use the following reasons: they want to save time, the crosswalks are out of the way, they can watch out for themselves and don't need crossing guards.)

What can we do to encourage all students to use the marked crosswalks? (The students might suggest awards for classrooms with the highest number of students who use the crosswalks; an individual reward, such as a sticker for those students using the crosswalks; penalties for students caught crossing in the middle of the street; and information about the number of people nationwide who are injured or killed when they do not cross at the marked intersections.)

2.   Acting Out Safe Pedestrian Behaviors

If you want young students to practice safe pedestrian behaviors when they are on their own, then they need to practice those behaviors first. Even such routine behaviors as looking both ways before crossing streets, looking for traffic turning at corners, and walking—not running—across streets at crosswalks take practice if the children are going to use them every time they cross the street.

You could design a skit for the students to act out or you might help the students design their own skits for practicing safe pedestrian behaviors. Some of the skits might target risky behaviors that are common among young children, such as running out into the street to chase a ball or a runaway pet, running into the street from between parked cars, or dashing across the street to meet a friend or a family member. Often, in these situations, the children do not realize that they are doing something that could have deadly consequences. They often do not think about or clearly understand cause-and-effect relationships. Acting out the positive and negative consequences of certain actions in skits might help them think first and thus prevent injuries.

Suggestions for Helping Younger Students Prevent Bicycling Injuries

1.   Reviewing Safe Bicycling Behaviors

Ask the students to complete the following sentence: "When I ride my bicycle, it's a good idea for me to..." List their suggestions on the board and find out how much they already know about preventing bicycling injuries. Then, ask how many of the students always follow the "It's a good idea for me to..." suggestions. Discuss why they do not always practice those behaviors, and talk about ways to make safe riding the "cool thing" to do. The following are some safe bicycling behaviors that you could share with the students if they do not suggest them.

When I ride my bicycle, it's a good idea for me to...

a.	Wear a bicycling helmet at all times and be sure the strap is fastened always. (To offer the best protection, the helmet should have a seal from the Snell Foundation or the American National Standards Institute (ANSI).)
b.	Observe all traffic rules and laws. Always be ready to yield the right of way. (Bicyclists should follow the same traffic rules as drivers of motor vehicles do: ride on the right side of the road with the traffic, not against the traffic; signal before every turn; obey all stop lights, stop signs, and yield signs; yield the right-of-way to pedestrians in crosswalks; do not ride on the sidewalks.)
c.	Keep to the right, as close to the curb as possible.
d.	Ride in a straight line, single file, when riding with others.
e.	Be sure I have a white headlight in good working order and at least one red reflector on the rear of my bicycle, if I must ride at night.

f.	Sound a horn or a bell to alert someone that I am riding by.
g.	Watch for cars pulling out into traffic from parking places and for people in parked cars who might open their doors suddenly.
h.	Never hitch onto other vehicles or perform stunts or race in traffic.
i.	Never carry riders on my bicycle. Carry packages in a basket, rack, or backpack. Except when signaling, keep my hands on the handlebars at all times.
j.	Be sure my bike is in safe mechanical condition.
k.	Stop at all intersections. Look both ways—left then right, then left again before crossing.

After the students review safe bicycling behaviors, you might present the following questions for discussion.

1. How might you prevent injuries while bicycling? (Emphasize that the best ways to prevent cycling injuries are to keep your bicycle in good repair, wear a bicycling helmet and proper clothing, and obey all traffic and safety rules.)

2. What parts of your bicycle should you and a responsible adult check for safety? (If you plan to use the next activity "Conducting a Bicycle Safety Check," postpone this discussion until then. If you do not plan to conduct that activity, then discuss the safety checkpoints noted in that activity.)

3. How safe are bicycling conditions in your neighborhood and around the school area? How could you and others at the school help to make the conditions safer? (The students should discuss such things as the traffic flow, the amount of traffic, safety of intersections for crossing streets, presence or absence of traffic lights or signs, and the maintenance of the streets, particularly the shoulders where the students would be riding.)

The students might end the lesson by designing posters that promote injury prevention while bicycling.

2. Conducting a Bicycle Safety Check

Bring a bicycle and a bicycling helmet into the classroom. Ask the students to suggest which parts of the bicycle they and their parents or guardians should check to be sure the bicycle is in good working order. Then, share with them a diagram similar to the following and point out each feature on the bicycle you brought to class. (If you want to use this illustration as your diagram, you may make a transparency of BLM 7.3 Is Your Bicycle in Shape? included in your teacher's guide.)

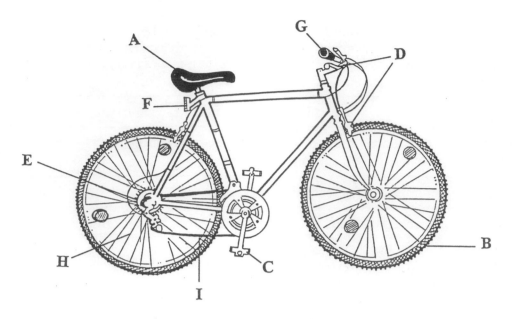

Show the students the bicycling helmet. Ask them if they know whether this helmet is a regulation helmet. If they do not know, show them the seal of approval from the Snell Foundation or the American National Standards Institute (ANSI). (Those two organizations can approve the materials and the structure of the helmet to ensure it will protect a bicyclist's head in the event of an impact with the pavement or another object.) The students should only buy and wear helmets that show the seal of approval.

Demonstrate how a helmet should be worn: evenly over the head, not tipped back; with the strap securely fastened so that the helmet cannot move easily from side to side or back and forth. Emphasize that an unfastened helmet cannot protect a rider's head because the helmet would fly off if the rider fell or ran into something.

3.   Setting up a Safety Inspection Station for Bicycles

Invite a bicycle repair person to the class and ask him or her to demonstrate good bicycle maintenance and the proper way to wear a helmet. Set up a bicycle inspection station at school where bicycle mechanics and knowledgeable adults can inspect the students' bicycles and their helmets. Have all the students bring their bicycles and helmets in for a safety check.

4.   Conducting a Safe Bicycling Awareness Day

You might plan and conduct a Safe Bicycling Awareness Day during which speakers could talk to the students about preventing injuries, bicycle mechanics could conduct safety checks, and the students could show their bicycling skill by riding through cycling checkpoints. The students could design plays, skits, or posters reminding others of bicycling behaviors that prevent injuries.

The following describes a sample course for a Bicycle Rodeo that you could lay out on the school grounds and use to test the students' bicycling skills. The course layout might include the following checkpoints (see sample course). You may use this design or design your own course:

⇒   the starting point where students show how to wear their helmets properly and how to get onto their bikes properly,
⇒   a corner to check knowledge of hand signals,
⇒   an obstacle course to check steering and handling ability,
⇒   a safe braking checkpoint,
⇒   a checkpoint to show proper mounting and dismounting and the height of the saddle,
⇒   a rough or sandy surface to test the ability to balance and steer in nonideal conditions.

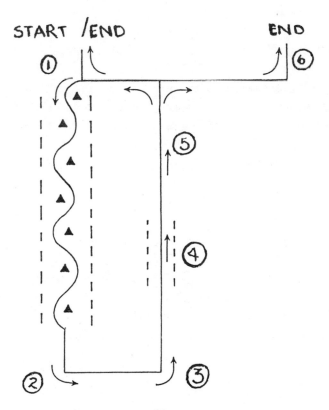

Suggestions for Helping Younger Students Prevent Injuries at Home

1.   Home, Safe Home?

Present the students with drawings (or models) of the inside and outside of a home that show some hazards that might cause injuries. (Your teacher has some drawings on BLM 7.4 in the teacher's guide that you could use for this task, or you could design your own drawings or models. A doll house might make a good model.)

First, instruct the students to place an "X" on the things they see in the illustrations (or to place red stickers on hazards in the models) that might cause injuries in or around this home. Next, have them add anything to the pictures (or models) that might prevent injuries in this home. (If there is not enough room in the picture to draw what they would like to show, they might write a description of the item or condition on the back of the drawing.)

Use the home survey you completed for ideas of possible hazards that might cause injuries and of items that help prevent injuries at home. For example, younger students probably will know that toys or books piled in stairways could cause someone to trip and fall, but they might not be aware that smoke alarms and fire extinguishers in the home help prevent injuries from fires.

2.   Speaking Out About Injury Prevention at Home

Arrange for a fire marshal or a volunteer from the American Red Cross to speak to your class about preventing injuries at home. Before the speaker arrives, have the students write questions they want to ask the visitor. Review the students' questions and encourage them to relate their questions to preventing injuries at home.

3.   How Safe Is My Home?

Distribute to the younger students the Home Injury-Prevention Survey that you completed in Preventing Injuries at Home. Discuss the survey with them and encourage them to complete the survey with family members at home that evening. (You might prepare a letter for the parents so that they understand the purpose of the survey.) After the students have returned their surveys, discuss their findings and the strategies the families plan to implement to prevent injuries at home.

WRAP UP

Discuss the following questions with your classmates.

1.   How did you feel about teaching younger students? Was it fun?—difficult?—rewarding?—stressful?
2.   What did you learn about preventing injuries as a result of teaching younger students?
3.   If you had the chance to teach younger students again, what would you do differently?—the same?

4.   What do you think was the most important thing the younger students learned? What was the most important thing **you** learned?

INVOLVING FAMILY MEMBERS

Take home the true/false quizzes on pedestrian and bicycling safety. How much do your family members know about walking and riding safely? Discuss what you could do as a family to reduce the possibility of injuries as pedestrians and bicyclists.

IF A STRANGER KNOCKS

In the United States today, one of the fastest growing violent crimes is sexual assault. Sexual assault victims are sometimes very young and sometimes very old, they can be of any age. Victims are males and females of every racial, ethnic, and socioeconomic group. No one is completely safe from sexual assault.

Perpetrators, the people who commit sexual assaults, see the crime as an act of violence, not of sex. Perpetrators interviewed in prison said most victims were not sexy to them at all. Rather, their victims were accessible and did not know how to protect themselves.

ACTIVITY: HOW CAN YOU PROTECT YOURSELF AGAINST SEXUAL ASSAULT?

Most people that you pass on the street or encounter during your daily activities have no intention of hurting anyone. Usually, they are people just like you going about their daily business. In dealing with strangers personally, you should be aware of what could happen and use strategies that will prevent any problems.

Perpetrators say that most victims make assault easy. They do foolish things and do not use common sense. When someone does not give the perpetrator a chance to attack, screams or yells, or resists assertively, the perpetrator usually leaves that person alone. The perpetrator then looks for an easier victim. How often do you do foolish things without using common sense? How would you react in situations that might be dangerous?

Each of the following scenes depicts the possibility for sexual assault or injury. What are some strategies you could use to prevent assault or injury in each case?

Procedure

1. With your teammates, read the scene that your teacher assigns.
2. Brainstorm possible responses for the young person in the scene.
    Record all the possible responses.
3. Select one response (from Step 2) that would be most likely to protect the young person from assault or injury.
4. Write that response in your notebook or on a piece of paper.
5. Decide how you will present the scene, including your final response, to the rest of the class.
    Decide who will take which roles and whether you need any props or a narrator. Decide if you want to change any of the dialogue.
6. Present your scene to your teacher and classmates.

SCENE #1: A PLEA FOR HELP

Lily is home alone when she hears a knock at the front door.

Stranger (knocking on closed door): "Hello, is anyone home?"
Lily (answers through the closed door): "Yes, what do you want?"
Stranger: "My car had a flat tire in front of your house. I don't have a spare. I need to use your telephone to call someone for help."

What should Lily do?

SCENE #2: AN OFFICIAL AT THE DOOR

Keith is home alone when he hears a knock at the front door.

Stranger (knocking on closed door): "Hello, is anyone home?"
Keith (answering through the closed door): "Who is it?"
Stranger: "I'm from the gas company. I need to read your meter for this month's bill."
Keith (opens the door a crack and sees a man in a gas company uniform): "I'm not sure I should let you in."
Stranger: "I have to get the reading from your gas meter in the basement. It's very important, and I cannot come back."

What should Keith do?

SCENE #3: IT'S AN EMERGENCY

Bob is home alone when he hears a knock at the front door.

Bob (opening the front door): "Yes."
Stranger: "Hello, I'm Mrs. Bowen. I work with your mom. She's had an accident at work and asked me to take you to the hospital. Your dad is already on the way there."

What should Bob do?

SCENE #4: A CALL FOR FAME AND FORTUNE

Michelle is home alone when the telephone rings.

Michelle (answering the telephone): "Hello."
Stranger: "Hello, this is Tom White of the Miles Stone Modeling Agency. Is your mother at home?"
Michelle: "No, she isn't."
Stranger: "Is your father there?"
Michelle: "No, he's at work."
Stranger: "Who is this?"
Michelle: "This is Michelle."
Stranger: "Michelle, I was actually calling to talk to you. I need someone to do some modeling for my agency. I called your school and the principal suggested that I call you. Would you like to be a model, Michelle? The salary is great."
Michelle: "I don't know."
Stranger: "Well, I need you this afternoon, and I could pick you up in five minutes. Have I found my model?"

What should Michelle do?

57

Rhonda and Diedre are walking home from school and notice a young man who appears to be following them. He is riding a motorcycle.

Rhonda (to Diedre): "Look at that cute guy on the motorcycle."
Diedre (elbowing Rhonda in the ribs): "Hey, he's coming our way."
Stranger (as he rides up to them): "Hi."
Rhonda and Diedre: "Hi yourself."
Stranger: "Do you two live around here?"
Rhonda (pointing in the direction of her apartment): "Yes, four blocks over on Blackstone."
Stranger: "It's a nice neighborhood."
Diedre (shrugging her shoulders): "It's okay."
Stranger (to Rhonda): "Would you like a ride home on my bike?" Rhonda hesitates.
Diedre (grinning and winking at Rhonda): "Oh, go on, Rhonda. I'll carry your books home."

What should Rhonda do?

Stop and Discuss

After all the teams present their scenes, critique the various responses and discuss the process your team went through in deciding which response was best.

1. How many possible solutions did your team list during the brainstorming session?
2. From your team's list, how did you decide which response to present to the class?
3. Which teams presented the best responses?
4. Why did you think those were the best? In other words, what criteria did you use to judge the effectiveness of the responses?
5. Can you think of other appropriate responses for the various scenes?

ACTIVITY: RESPONDING ASSERTIVELY TO LURES

Sex offenders often lure young victims away from the safety of home or a group. (A lure is something that tempts or attracts someone with the promise of getting a reward or something the person wants.) The five scenes you acted out illustrate typical lures used by sex offenders to find a victim. Convicted sex offenders report how easy it is to find victims because many young people act first and think later. Most offenders reported that if they were questioned or openly confronted by a young person, they backed off and looked for someone else. Assertive actions were the best prevention strategies.

What are assertive actions? Assertive actions are those that show you are willing to stand up for yourself and not become a victim. Some assertive actions are the following: say "no!" or "get away from me!" in a loud voice, walk quickly away from a person who makes you feel uncomfortable, clearly refuse to get into a car or to take something from someone who makes you feel uncomfortable, call for help if you find yourself in a situation that you cannot handle, or firmly push a person away if he or she tries to touch you.

Procedure

1. Working in teams of two or three, create some fictitious but realistic situations similar to the scenes you acted out during this lesson.
    Think about where students your age might be confronted, such as at the mall, on your way home from school, or at the skating rink.
2. Write out a script for a possible lure, but do not provide an ending.
3. After you finish your script, trade with another team.
4. Provide an assertive response to end the script you received from the other team.
5. Then, either read your ending, or act out the entire scene for the class.

WRAP UP

After you have presented all the scripts, decide on the best assertive responses for the various situations and list those on the board. Practice those responses with your classmates. You might need to use them sometime!

INVOLVING FAMILY MEMBERS

Share the scenes from this lesson with your parents or guardians. Ask them what they think the young person should do in each case and share the results from your class discussion. Discuss the procedures your parents or guardians want you to follow if you are every home alone and someone should knock on your door.

IT'S AN EMERGENCY!

READING: THINK BEFORE YOU BABYSIT

Judy, about to leave the house on the way to her babysitting job, was annoyed when her mother called for her to wait. "Be sure you get the phone number where the Tylers will be. Remember, we won't be home tonight, so you'll definitely need to know how to reach them."

Judy, one step out the door, said, "Yes, I'll remember."

"…and be sure you know all about Joey's medicine. Ann Tyler told me this morning that he still had a cough."

"I know, I know," replied Judy, and with a wave, she was off.

When she arrived at the Tylers, they were eager to be on their way, and after exchanging a few words, they left. Judy's mind was on a phone call she had forgotten to make before she left home. As soon as the Tyler's car pulled out of the driveway and Judy was convinced that Joey was playing happily on the floor, she dialed her friend.

Suddenly, she heard a shrill scream. She dropped the phone and ran into the living room. Joey had apparently taken a cigarette lighter from the table and lit it, burning his right hand badly. He was screaming in pain.

Judy panicked. She held Joey, trying to comfort him, but realized she did not know what to do next. She ran to the kitchen to find the phone number of Joey's parents, but they had forgotten to write it down on the noteboard and she had forgotten to ask. She thought of calling her parents, but remembered they weren't home. She looked at Joey's burned, blistered hand and felt helpless.

A nightmare—the injury of the child in a babysitter's care—had happened, and Judy had just realized she was unprepared for this emergency. Before you go to babysit, ask yourself some important questions. First, do you know the basics of first aid? All babysitters should, because children may be hurt during play, or become ill while in your care. Second, ask the parents the following questions:

☎ Where can they be reached?
☎ Where are the telephone numbers of the doctor, the fire department, poison control center, and a trusted neighbor? Also, you should know the location of the family's first aid supplies, fire extinguisher, and the primary electrical box. If the child is on medication, you should ask how often and how much of the medicine you should give the child. After asking these questions, you are ready to assume responsibility for a child.

Good first aid begins with prevention. When you are on your own with the child, be alert to these potential hazards:

▶▶ If there are gates on stairways to prevent falls, are they securely closed?
▶▶ Are there any lighters or matches within the child's reach?
▶▶ Do any of the child's toys have sharp edges or points or parts that could be pulled off and swallowed?
▶▶ Are all plastic bags out of reach?
▶▶ Are all doors locked?
▶▶ Are there any spills that should be wiped up to keep you or the child in your care from slipping?
▶▶ Are all potential poisons out of the child's reach?

Once the surroundings are safe, you can settle down to play with the child and not talk on the phone. Children require 100 percent of your attention because they quickly can get into mischief.

Despite all of your precautions, a child in your care still could be injured. Then, you must know what to do and where to find first-aid supplies.

READING: CALLING FOR HELP

Would you know what to do in an emergency situation like the one Judy faced? Would you know who to call, or how to keep someone who is seriously injured alive until help arrived? This lesson cannot tell you all you need to know, but it will give you some tips for dealing with medical emergencies. In most cases, you should not try to treat someone yourself unless the person is bleeding severely or is not breathing. The best emergency procedure is a call for help. Most cities and towns in the United States use the 911 emergency medical service. (In some areas, the 911 service is not available, and people must dial a seven-digit number to get help. If your area does not have 911 service, look for your special emergency number for your area.) After you dial 911 (or your special emergency number) on the telephone, a dispatcher answers. After finding out about the emergency, the dispatcher notifies the people best prepared to help you—the police, the fire department, an ambulance service, the poison control center, or a hospital. Usually, when people call 911 or any emergency medical service, they are upset, nervous, and want someone to help them in a hurry. Sometimes, they cannot remember what they must tell the dispatcher so that he or she can send help right away. An easy way to remember what to tell the emergency medical service dispatcher is to remember the word L-I-F-E. Using L-I-F-E might help you save a life! L-I-F-E stands for:

L=LOCATION

Where did the injuries occur? Give the street address, if possible, or the street names at the closest intersection.

I=INJURIES

How did the person get hurt? Which parts of the person's body are injured? Describe the injuries as specifically as you can. Is there more than one victim?

F=FIRST AID

How is the victim already being helped? What else should be done?

E=EQUIPMENT

What special pieces of equipment might be needed, such as a ladder, a rope, special chemicals for fires or hazardous spills, or tools to get someone out of a vehicle or out from under something?

Talk slowly and clearly with the dispatcher. The dispatcher must know where you are and what the problem is to send help. Do not hang up on the dispatcher, you might forget to give some important information. Let the dispatcher hang up first, and then wait for help.

ACTIVITY: PRACTICING L-I-F-E

Procedure

1.   Think of an emergency situation for which someone might need to call 911.
2.   Practice with a partner calling 911 and giving the dispatcher the appropriate information. *Your partner will play the role of the dispatcher when you place your call. Then, you will*

play the role of the dispatcher when your partner places a call.

3. Critique your performances.
Did you remember all the important information? Did you follow the L-I-F-E guidelines?

ACTIVITY: HELPING THE HARMED

Procedure

1. Read about each of the following injuries.
2. Besides calling for help, write what you think would be the most helpful action or actions you could take for each injury.
3. Then, write something that someone might do that could make the injury worse.

Injury #1: Baby Bonita burned her hand with a cigarette lighter.

Injury #2: Curious Carla swallowed some "medicine" that turned out to be poisonous.

Injury #3: Eat-in-a-rush Eddie got a piece of food stuck in his windpipe and could not breathe.

Injury #4: In-line skating Ian fell as he was skating, hit his head on the pavement, and knocked himself out.

Injury #5: Woodworker Wanda cut her hand very deeply with a sharp knife, the cut was bleeding a lot.

Injury #6: Outdoor Otto was stung by a bee, and he might be allergic to bee stings.

Stop and Discuss

1. How much do you and your classmates know about emergency first aid procedures?
2. Are there differences of opinion about what should be done and what should not be done for each injury?
3. How could you find out which are the appropriate procedures to follow in each case?

READING: YOU CAN'T WAIT

In general, three emergency conditions require immediate care. Those conditions are severe bleeding, stopped breathing, and poisoning. Being untreated for even a few minutes could mean death for the victim.

What should you do in those emergency situations? The following are recommendations from the American Red Cross as described in *American Health*, March 1992.

<u>For Severe Bleeding</u>

Have someone call 911 (or the emergency medical service number in your area) while you apply direct pressure to the wound by placing a gauze pad or clean cloth firmly over it. (By using a barrier such as a cloth, you can help avoid transmission of any infectious diseases spread by blood-

65

to-blood contact.) Elevate the injured area, continuing to apply direct pressure, unless the elevation causes pain. Maintain direct pressure at all times. If you and the victim are alone and if it is possible, have the victim maintain pressure on the wound at this point while you call 911.

Cover the cloth or pad with a bandage, tie or tape the bandage in place. If blood soaks through, do not remove the original cloths and bandages. Add more pads and bandages over the original ones. If a body part, such as a finger or toe, has been amputated, wrap the severed part in a clean cloth and place it inside a plastic bag. Keep the severed part cold until the ambulance personnel arrive. Do not pack it in ice.

For Stopped Breathing

If the victim is choking...

If the person has stopped breathing due to choking, have someone call 911 while you do the Heimlich maneuver (abdominal thrusts). To perform the Heimlich maneuver, stand behind the victim and place the thumb side of your fist against the person's abdomen, just above the navel and below the ribs. Grab the fist with your other hand and give quick, upward thrusts into the abdomen until the obstruction is removed, or until emergency personnel arrive.

If you are alone with the victim, do several thrusts. If you fail to dislodge the blockage, call 911. If you are choking, give yourself abdominal thrusts by bending over and pressing your abdomen onto the back of a chair or some other firm object.

If the person is not breathing for any other reason...

If the person has stopped breathing for another reason, act quickly! Have someone call 911 and place the victim on his or her back. Tilt the head back and lift the chin. This opens the airway by moving the tongue away from the back of the throat. Pinch the nose shut, seal your lips around the person's mouth and give two breaths, just enough to make the person's chest rise.

If your breaths do not go into the person's lungs, the airway could be blocked. Retilt the person's head and give two more breaths. If breaths still do not go in, there is probably an object blocking the air passage. Place the heel of your hand against the middle of the person's abdomen, put your other hand on top of the first and press upward into the person's abdomen six to 10 times. Look in the mouth and use your finger to sweep out any object you see. Check again for breathing and a pulse.

If there is a pulse but the person is still not breathing on his or her own, continue mouth-to-mouth (rescue) breathing, giving one breath every five seconds. If you are alone with the victim, call 911 after one minute (12 breaths), then resume rescue breathing. Check for a pulse and breathing every minute.

If there is no pulse...

If you are alone with the victim, do one minute of CPR (cardiopulmonary resuscitation), then call 911. Otherwise, have someone else call 911 while you begin CPR. Place your hands in the center of the chest and compress the chest about 1½ to 2 inches for an adult (not as deep for

66

children). Do this 15 times. Then give two breaths. Repeat this sequence three more times and then recheck for a pulse. If there is still no pulse, continue CPR until the emergency personnel arrive.

If someone is unconscious...

If you think someone is unconscious, tap the victim and shout, "Are you okay?" If there is no response, then gently tilt the person's head back and lift the chin. This opens the airway by moving the tongue away from the back of the throat. Check for breathing by looking at the chest to see if it is rising, listen and feel at the nose and mouth for breathing. If the person is not breathing on his or her own, then use rescue breathing techniques.

For Suspected Poisoning

Quickly survey the surroundings to find out what type of poison was ingested (look for objects, such as empty medicine bottles or household cleanser containers). If you suspect an inhaled poison, such as carbon monoxide, get the person into fresh air and call 911.

If the person is conscious and you know the poison ingested a corrosive or caustic substance such as ammonia, immediately give the person sips of water or milk to dilute the poison, do not induce vomiting. Since the information on the poison's container may be outdated, call 911 and the poison control center, and follow the dispatcher's directions.

What about Outdoor Otto who was stung by a bee? First, you should look for a stinger. If you see one, remove it by scraping it away with your fingernail or a plastic card or by using tweezers. Wash the area with soap and water, and apply a cold pack to reduce swelling. To reduce pain and itching, apply calamine lotion or a water and baking soda paste. Watch for signs of an allergic reaction for about 30 minutes. If someone is allergic to bee stings (or any other insect bite), they will show some or all of the following symptoms: difficulty breathing, tightness of the throat or chest, severe itching, swelling of the tongue or mouth, nausea, and dizziness. If a reaction occurs, or if you know that someone is allergic to bee stings or other insect bites and that person's medicine is not handy, then call 911 right away or get the person to a medical facility.

READING: MORE BABYSITTING BASICS

Here's a little more information for those of you who might be caring for younger children.

Cuts and Scrapes

Kids can fall down, run into things, and get hit with things. The result is often a minor wound. Any wound should be washed thoroughly with soap and water, then rinsed. Let it air dry or blot it dry with sterile gauze, if it is available. If the parents have said it is permissible, you can use a first aid ointment, otherwise simply cover the wound with an adhesive bandage.

If bleeding from a wound does not stop within 5 minutes after washing, try applying direct pressure to the wound with a sterile gauze pad. Hold the wound above the heart and press for 5 minutes—without peeking at it. It may take that long for a clot to form. Then, leave the gauze in place and apply a bandage or tape over it. If you remove the gauze, you could disturb the clot, and bleeding may resume. If bleeding cannot be controlled with these measures, or involves a serious cut to the head, call for help.

Burns

Even though you take every precaution, active children may burn themselves, often with tap water that is too hot. Initially, you must determine the degree of burn. First-degree burns are red and painful. Second-degree burns—which is what Joey had—have blisters, and third-degree burns are charred or white. First- and second-degree burns can be treated with cold water to relieve the pain. You may need to apply cold water for a long time before the pain stops. Take care not to break blisters. Then, cover the burn with sterile gauze.

If a child's clothing catches on fire, the procedure is "stop, drop, and roll." This means stop the child from running, place him on the floor, wrap a blanket around him, and roll him to smother the flames. Call for emergency help immediately.

Poisons

Poisoning is a major threat to small children. Poisons can be swallowed, inhaled, splashed into the eyes, or burn the skin. Your first step is to identify the poison. Then, call a poison control center and get instructions.

In case of a severe emergency, such as a house fire, remember that your first responsibility is the safety of the child or children. Gather them and leave the house.

A babysitter who thinks ahead, comes prepared, and asks the right questions can make the difference between a serious injury and the prevention of an injury altogether. Remember, a child's life is in your hands.

WRAP UP

Invite to your classroom a guest speaker from the American Red Cross or another organization that deals with emergency medical situations. Before the speaker arrives, write some questions you have about emergency medical procedures and when to use them. Plan to demonstrate for the guest speaker some of the procedures you learned during this lesson, and ask the guest for suggestions that will improve your performance.

INVOLVING FAMILY MEMBERS

If much of the information in this lesson is new to you or if you are unsure if you could perform the tasks described, then you should take a basic first aid course from a reputable organization such as the American Red Cross. Because everyone needs to know first aid, you could suggest that family members take the course with you, or maybe you or your teacher could arrange for such a course to be taught at school for students and their families. Preventing injuries is the first priority, but then you need to know what to do if injuries happen.

LESSON 10

MAKING INJURY PREVENTION
A SCHOOL PRIORITY

How safe are you and other students from injuries at school? According to national statistics, approximately 22,000 students are injured at school or during school-sponsored activities every year. How often are students, teachers, or visitors injured at your school or at school-sponsored events? What can be done to make your school and school grounds an injury-free zone?

ACTIVITY: IDENTIFYING DANGER ZONES

Procedure

1. Take a mental tour of the inside and the outside of your school and think about places in or around the school where someone could be injured.

2. Either by yourself or with a partner, make a list on notebook paper of the locations in or around the school where you think someone could be injured.
    Include the school grounds and all areas where school activities take place, including the gym and practice areas for sports.

3. With your classmates and teacher, tour the school and the school grounds. Use your list from step 2 to help guide you through the school.

4. As you walk around, look for additional places where someone could be injured and add those locations to your list.
    Consider the possible environmental factors and human factors that might make injuries more likely.

5.   After you return to the classroom, write the specific problem related to each location you listed.
You might organize your list into two columns.

Location	Related Problem
Stairwell	Papers on stairs, someone could slip and fall.
Leaking Water Fountain	Someone could slip in the water on the floor.

ACTIVITY: INJURIES AT SCHOOL

Now that you have identified some possible locations where students, teachers, or school visitors could be injured at school, what else should you know if your goal is to prevent injuries at school or at school-sponsored events? You might want to know how many students, teachers, or visitors are actually injured at your school or at school-sponsored activities each week and where those injuries occurred. You also might want to know how serious the injuries were.

Procedure

1.   Decide how you could keep track of all the injuries that happen in the school building, on the school grounds, or at school-sponsored events for one week.
     You might organize your information in a data table.
2.   Decide what information you need to record.
     You might want to record the type of injury, the location of the injury, the age of the injured person, whether the injury was caused by human or environmental factors or both, and the seriousness of the injury, for example.
3.   Create a data table or another means of keeping track of your information.
4.   Share with classmates your idea from step 3 for recording the data.
5.   As a class, decide on the best way to record information on injuries that happen in or around the school. Also, decide what information you should record and how you will get that information.
     You might enlist the help of the principal and the school nurse.
6.   For one week, record all the injuries that occur in or around the school and at school-sponsored events.

Stop and Discuss

1.   What hazards (environmental factors) did you find during your tour of the school and school grounds?
2.   How could the environment be improved?
3.   What types of injuries occurred most often at school?
4.   Where did most of those injuries occur?
5.   Was there any relationship between the injuries reported and the environmental factors you identified in question #1?

WRAP UP

During this unit, you have learned about the causes of unintentional injuries and death primarily among young people. Also, you have talked a lot about ways to prevent unintentional injuries as a pedestrian, as a bicyclist, at home, at school, in a motor vehicle, and if approached by a stranger. Now, you will have an opportunity to share with your peers what you have learned.

To show what you have learned about preventing injuries among young people, work with your classmates in designing an Injury-Prevention Campaign. How might you convince your peers that preventing injuries is important? Many students have the attitude that "it won't happen to me." Is there any way that you can change that attitude and help other students realize that they could be injured, and even die, if they take unnecessary risks?

You might plan a display, have an "Injury-Prevention" party, or write a play. The choice is up to you. Your job is to help your friends stay alive and injury free.

INVOLVING FAMILY MEMBERS

Invite family members to view your displays, skits, plays, or other products of your Injury-Prevention Campaign. Find out if your family members have changed their behavior regarding safety belt use, home safety, or injury-prevention strategies as a result of their involvement in this injury-prevention unit.

ACKNOWLEDGMENTS

"To Risk" on p. 20 is reprinted from *The Changer and The Changed* by N. Dimella and C. Bershad with permission of the publisher, Learning for Life/Management Sciences for Health. Copyright 1981.

"Think Before You Babysit" on pp. 61-62 and 67-68 is reprinted from the November 1989 issue of *Current Health 2* magazine with permission of the publisher, Weekly Reader Corporation. Copyright 1989.

"Calling for Help" on pp. 62-63 is adapted from "The Call for Help" in the November 1988 issue of *Current Health 2* magazine with permission of the publisher, Weekly Reader Corporation. Copyright 1988.

"You Can't Wait" on pp. 65-67 is adapted from "Life Savers" in the March 1992 issue of *American Health*, by Lisa Braen McGrath. Copyright 1992.